# LOVE AND LONGING

## YEARNING FOR THE FACE OF GOD

SUKINA
NOOR

RADIANT HEART BOOKS

*And to God belongs the east and the west. So wherever you turn, there is the Face of God. Indeed, God is all-Encompassing and Knowing.*

*Quran 2:115*

*And keep yourself patient with those who call upon their Lord in the morning and the evening seeking His Face. And let not your eyes pass beyond them, desiring adornments of the worldly life.*

*Quran 18:28*

*Everyone upon the earth will perish, and the Face of your Lord full of Majesty and Honour will abide forever.*

*Quran 55:26-27*

# LOVE AND LONGING
## YEARNING FOR THE FACE OF GOD

Published by Radiant Heart Books

# *Praise for Love and Longing: Yearning for the Face of God*

This collection is evidence of an unceasing realization of the divine reality within the Islamic spiritual tradition of Islamic mysticism or Sufism. The author's arresting language speaks to the universal truths of the human condition, both the emptiness of insatiable longing for the infinite being of God, and the unfathomable intimacy of the overflowing divine manifestation, represented in God's statement to the Prophet Muhammad, blessings and peace upon him, "I am not contained in My heavens or on My earth, but I am contained in the heart of my faithful servant." *Love and Longing* will awaken the seeker from his slumber, and the work will serve as an important addition to any curriculum in the study of contemporary Sufism.

**Dr Zachary Wright,** Professor of History and Religious Studies, Northwestern University in Qatar. Author of *Realizing Islam: the Tijaniyya in North Africa and the 18th Century Muslim World.*

Sukina's verses bear a spiritual sensuality, enticing city dwellers from London to LA, transporting us to sacred, secret lands, sometimes far in distance but in reality so near, unveiling the Face of God within and in the hearts of mystics and lovers with whom we walk the way to God. As Sukina invites us into the most intimate spaces, we discover a seeker and teacher so warm, so giving, we know for sure she wants for us what her own soul has tasted and still yearns.

**Dr Jamillah Karim**, author of *Women of the Nation: Between Black Protest and Sunni Islam* and *American Muslim Women: Negotiating Race, Class, and Gender Within the Ummah.*

In this important collection of her poems, Sukina Noor picks up the pen of Rabia al-Adawiyya (d. 801 CE) that has been passed down to us through a chain and generations of luminary and phenomenal women poets like A'isha al-Ba'uniyya (d. 1517 CE), Nana Asma'u (d. 1864 CE), Mwana Kupona (d. 1865 CE), to mention only these few.

**Shaykh Michael Mumisa** PhD candidate and Cambridge Special Livingstone Scholar, University of Cambridge. Author of *Introducing Arabic* and *Islamic Law: Theory and Interpretation.*

Through her devastatingly delightful devotion to the vulnerable expression of her own heart's truths, Sukina holds up a squeaky clean mirror to the eyes of the reader, through which our own quests for belonging, purpose and knowledge of ourselves as human emanations of the Divine can be seen, studied and celebrated. This text is a boldly sacred one. Noor's words moved me in the same way I have been moved by the words of ancient mystics, yet simultaneously swayed my heart to the modern rhythms of the cultures and life experiences that have informed her unique, soulful voice.

**Yaya Da Costa,** actress *Chicago Med* and *Our Kind of People.*

This book is a junction between the two seas, a light that is neither from the West nor the East reflecting the teachings of her Grand Shaykh, Sidi Ibrahim Niass as a synthesis of all the sound Sufi traditions. In her verses one could sense the Rumian harmony in another an Akbarian riddle, the whole collection honey-coated in the gnostic syllabus only known to the initiated ones, giving us a clear portrait of its writer. Born and bred in the Western world, she was able to set herself free from its castles of concrete and set ablaze her carnal self and like a phoenix in the West, soar towards the skyscrapers of mystic love. This book is not mere poetry, it's a journey to the lands of sainthood, wayfaring to the tavern of wisdom where brethren drink to the remembrance of the beloved from the cup of eternal love. The beauty of the poetry is bedazzling and this collection has it all; the rhythm, the melodies and above an everlasting spirit.

**Cheikh Ahmed Boukar Niang,** author of *The Sincere Aspirant* and translator of *Sayrul Qalb* and *Nurul Haqq*, poetry collections of Shaykh Ibrahim Niasse.

Poet and cultural icon Sukina Noor's debut poetry collection, is like a balm that has arrived just as the world is in need of intense spiritual healing. The volume is full of affirmation, celebration, and reconnection. The poems are not only reflective, they are instructive, calling us to look deeper into our relationship with Allah. It is poetry that is both grounded and pure; it is a spiritual awakening in verse. From the reminders in "If Only You Knew" and "Woman of God" to the beautiful longing in "Invitation", this is a book that you will run to again and again. Love and Longing: Yearning for the Face of God is an opening and a celebration of abiding love.

**Angelica Lindsay Ali,** Community Scholar and founder of The Village Aunty Institute.

Part invocation, part affirmation, these are the words and prayers of someone who has been turned around on the path so many times that she knows the way home by heart. This work feels both ancient and futuristic, but only because it has that quality of presence that allows it to be timeless. Each word is full of life and sweet nectar for the soul. These messages are gentle reminders of the level of access that we all have to something greater than ourselves, but that we are ultimately not separate from. Sukina shows us that her relationship with language, the vibration of words and speaking truth are a spiritual technology. That quality of witnessing someone who honours their gifts through mastering their craft is an inspiration in and of itself. There are many individual lessons here and a generous amount of wisdom. But the commitment to reverence and honouring the sacred is what won me over.

**Maryam Hasnaa** founder of New Earth Mystery School.

This offering is as intimate and generous and as true as any of us can hope to be. By reading it, you know what it is to know a seeker. At one, in The One.

**Brother Ali, Rapper**, *The Undisputed Truth, Mourning in America* and *Dreaming in Color*.

Sukina is a contemporary mystic poet whose words surround us like divine caress. Her words pulse with both the yearning for, and the presence of, the Beloved. Her poetry drips with devotion to the Sacred Presence and beckons us to draw near. *Love and Longing* is a soulful caress that reminds us there is nothing but the Beloved. Sukina writes in the ancient tradition of the Sufi mystic poets, and her words themselves are dhikr. In this brilliant manuscript, she embraces the deepest yearn, while simultaneously, lushly quenching it. *Love and Longing* shimmers with brilliant devotion, as it calls us stunningly home.

**Taya Ma Shere** co-founder of Kohenet Hebrew Priestess Institute and co-author of *The Hebrew Priestess: Ancient and New Visions of Jewish Women's Spiritual Leadership.*

Sukina has provided a thought-provoking dialogue, spiritual beauty through her poetry. Reading her poems has become a daily ritual for me, an affirmation for me to begin my day, a way for me to check in with my heart enabling me to understand my inner-self a little more. Being able to talk about her spiritual life whilst in the inner city so candidly makes her poetry stand above so many others. She is real, she feels what I feel, she lives how I live. She speaks from the heart.

**Beverley Douglas,** author of *Cutie.*

Sukina Noor is talking to our hearts. She has generously opened up her heart to let us in, to give us a peep of a heart that is running to Allah, so intensely. This heart is sometimes stuck in the middle of the city but it always finds a way to point towards Allah. Enjoy-Indulge-Taste

**Rakin Fetuga Niasse** author of *Third Eye Open.*

*Love and Longing* is an intimate and captivating conversation of spiritual awakening. Sukina Noor speaks to the readers of nothing but God and everything through God. With a yearning so palpable it ignites the same emotion in the readers, these poems and reflections show what is possible for contemporary Sufi poetry; how the voice of the present can speak of God and invite everyone to experience Divine love. Amongst the beauty, the book is honest about the world, the start of a spiritual journey and what it is like to eagerly approach the unknown.

**Rakaya Fetuga**, poet, *Letters to the Earth* and *SLAM: You're Gonna Wanna Hear This.*

*O Allah, make my heart present in your Holy Presence forever.
And ever.*

# Contents

# Author's Welcome

Dear Beloved,

You are welcome here. Make yourself comfortable as I take you on a journey into the chambers of my heart. I am grateful that you have chosen to walk with me. You are holding in your hand pieces of my soul, I present them to you as an offering. Pull up a chair and feast on these words from a woman in pursuit of nearness to God. If the Rose on the front cover represents my heart, then each of these poems are its petals. It's an honour to share them with you.

These poems were written at the beginning of my spiritual journey, although a woman of faith before, there was a point when the journey deepened. What can I say other than, I wanted more. The outward aspects of my faith tradition satisfied my limbs but my spirit was still thirsty. There had to be more to this faith thing. There had to be healing and joy and tears flowing from His Mercy; there had to be proximity and laughter and dancing in the rain. I came upon a spiritual path that made my desire for God a possibility. My heart hasn't been the same since.

These poems are the outpourings from the moment when the journey truly began. When these poems emerged, they were different to anything I had written before. I wasn't writing for an audience, I was writing because my heart was waking up and I had no choice but to get these words out. They were bursting out of my chest like shooting stars. I call them poems but in truth they are my heart's overflow. An experience, a moment, a reflection shared in poem form.

When I read over the poems, I can feel the state of my heart, the fire of longing and the desire for nothing else but the One who breathed His Spirit into me. Most of these poems were written in London where the journey began, so this is the story of a soul seeking God in the city. Dwelling in a place that points to everything but God, here I was seeking nothing but God. Desiring a nearness to Him in all spaces, seeking His Face in all faces.

It is important for me to share these poems because I want other souls to know that the pursuit of God isn't a feature of a bygone era. The journey isn't only reserved for pious people in holy lands who don't have flaws and never make mistakes, who never take a wrong turn and never listen to the whispers of their lower selves. No, this journey is for everyone; don't let some person in religious robes tell you otherwise. The door to the Divine Presence is open. God's Mercy covers us all. These poems are expressions of an everyday person in pursuit of God and if I can walk the path then so can you.

At times I would question myself, who I am to pursue God the way mystics of the past had done? Who do I think am I to walk this path and utter the things I do in these poems? Until the question became, Who am I not to? Who am I not to seek the Source of my spirit and the Moulder of my body? Who am I not to seek freedom from this fading world of flesh and forms? Who am I not to seek the Truth? These poems are the audacity of an ordinary woman who dared to pursue the Face of God.

My highest intention for this collection is that these words inspire you to embark upon your own voyage towards Truth, whatever that looks like for you. If you have already set out on your journey, may these poems serve as a reminder that you are not alone, that you are part of a caravan of seekers. If your journey has paused, may this be the reminder for you to continue your pursuit. The journey is not always easy but it is, without a doubt, wonderful. *Seek God because He wants to be found* my dear teacher would say.

The same way Rose petals are spread to welcome the presence of a lover, may these petals be spread across your heart as you welcome the Presence of The Source of all Love and Beauty.

Love always,

Sukina Noor

June 2022

So wherever you turn, there is the Face of Allah.

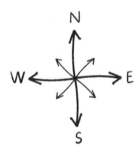

# Dear Beloved

Dear Beloved
You are welcome here
Make yourself comfortable
You will be warm around my fire
All that I have is yours
All that I am, an open door
A tray with spiced tea
Dates and sweet grapes
I offer you all of myself
Because in reality
I am nothing
But a conversation
Between God and Himself.
I am a collection of His attributes
Woven with this flesh
Like a Persian rug set
To create this being; human.
What do I own
That was not a gift from Him?
This breath
These eyes
This heart
Fixed into my chest
With words that spring forth
From the world of spirit, gifted.
Beloved, draw near
You are welcome here.

# The Stars Began to Burn

The stars began to burn
Outside your window
Restless and eager
For your voyage to begin.
You didn't realise
Their glisten
Was an invitation
For you to shine
So brightly
The sun would bow
In reverence.
They glow all night
Just waiting for you
To awaken to your greatness.
Spit your fears
Into the cosmos
Bury your shadows
Under the oak tree
And come.
They want to dance with you
And teach you
How to waltz freedom
How to bleed light
And shine
With no fear of
Of dimming .
Even though it hurts
And your house in burning
And your stomach is churning
And you feel like giving up
And you feel like throwing up
They want to teach you
How to set the heavens ablaze
Anyway.

They want to show you
How to turn your body
Into a lantern
So your inner flame
Can flicker
And make patterns
On the walls.
The stars outside your window
Are blazing
Just for you
Inviting you
To discard yesterday
And not waste time
Contemplating on a tomorrow
That may never come.
They want to show you
How to glow
Gloriously
Right now.
Right now, Beloved
And pursue the path
Towards Truth.

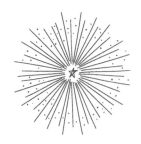

# Honour your Truth

Honour your truth
Hold it close to your chest
Like a new born baby.
Find your voice
And sing freedom songs
To your own soul
To help it grow.
Greet trees with dignity
Tread the Earth gently
And give birth
To brighter tomorrows
Every morning.
Learn the language of the stars
And the cycles of the moon
Strive to see the sunset
It will give you hope
When the darkness lingers.
Speak with mercy in your throat
And truth between your teeth
Have compassion in your eyes
Gentleness upon your fingertips
And God's Names upon your lips
Rub them in like mango-scented lip balm.
Speak with your heart
Listen to your intuition
And look beyond
The veils of separation
Until there are no veils
Or notions of separation
Until all that exists is the One.
Treat everyone
As though they are a Friend of God
With a secret for you
Hidden in their chest.

Daydream often
Drift on them
To lands unseen.
Angels are always with you.
Remember that.
Fall in love
With your Prophet ﷺ
So deeply
That only God
Can catch you.
Sit with scholars of the Sacred
Seek out the knowers
Hang out with the lovers
Who graze in God's Garden
And are present in His Presence
With every breath.
Never leave their side child
Not for the world and all it contains.
Sit amongst them
Until you become them.
Go on pilgrimages
Even in your own city
Make every journey a voyage
To He who is ever so close.
Keep a dream diary
Breathe fully
Make art
Wage love
And smile at everyone.
Pray intimately
Even for your enemies.
Love hard
With a soft heart
So full, It could burst
Across the galaxy
At any moment.
Honour your truth.

Listen to a recording
of this poem here

5

# Writing Myself into Existence

I have spent my entire life
Trying to wrap words
Around my existence.
Spent my early teens
Trying to find the purpose
That has been hidden in me.
Tried to find words
To help me unearth
My higher purpose.
Stood under spotlights
Found a home behind the mic
Leaking words into the night
Hurling my heart upon the sky
Searching for insight
Seeking out my tribe
Pursuing mirrors in people
So I could see my reflection
In someone else's eyes.
A generation of lost ones
Trying to be found ones
We know we are more
Than what this dense world
Of forms, would have us believe
So we look up to the stars
Hoping they can help us
Find our way back home.
Here, castles of concrete
Suffocate the skyline
And the street lights
Drown out the heavenly bodies
I rarely see the stars anymore;
Imagine if God wanted to inform us
Of the coming of a Prophet-child
In a manger somewhere in Palestine
We all would have missed the memo.

This world of loss and heartache
Shaped my inner landscape
But my soul desperately aches
For a land beyond the rainbow
Beyond the density of this *Dunya*
A realm that makes this mess
Make sense, you know?
I spoke my truth into being
Hoping someone was listening
That they would whisper in my ear
*Beloved, I hear you.*
I used verse to reintroduce
My heart to the universe.
Used words to communicate
A reality so unbearably great
That even the cosmos collaborates
To help us find our way back home.
We scribble symbols on paper
Hoping these marks can translate
The stories curled up
In the corners of our hearts.
We yearn to relay an ancient story
That every soul is trying to recall.
Restless whilst the world rests
Our hearts glow inside our chests
Hoping our words will spark hearts
To embark upon a voyage
Towards a Truth so pure
Falsehood runs out the door
Never to be seen again.

# Everyone is Hurting

Everyone is hurting
Suffering in some way
Missing someone
Battling some insecurity
Subduing some fear
Praying for change to come
Nursing open wounds
Invisible to the naked eye.
We all carry burdens on our back
We are all in desperate need of healing
From trauma and heartbreak and abuse
And our separation from the sweetness of
God.
So how about
Even if just for today
We try be good to each other
The kind of good that washes
Over your body like shooting stars
That awakens butterflies in stomachs
And makes joy a possibility
And hope an option
Even if just for today.
A small act of kindness
Can be the difference
Between heaven and hell
For the ones whose heart
Is leaking blood into the ocean.
For the Love of God
Let us give love
Even if the recipient
Is simply ourselves.

# Prayer / Poem

Sometimes
I don't know the difference
Between Prayer and Poem
And I am wondering
If maybe they are relatives
Or something.
With both
My heart seems
To expand
W i d e r
Than the chest
It sits in
Heart-arms growing
Out of my torso
To touch
The core
Of whoever cares to listen.
In my silence
There is a door
I glide through
To gain access
To an enchanted
World of words
Where both Prayer
And Poetry
Invite me to stay a while
As they narrate stories
Beneath a moonlit sky.
Prayer taught me
How to speak to God
How to be intimate
With the Holy Architect
How to whisper sweet nothings
Whilst in prostration
To the Hand-Crafter of Creation.

Prayer said;
*Speak not from the tongue*
*In your mouth*
*But from the tongue*
*In your heart.*
*The Most High*
*Always replies*
She said with a glint
In her eyes
*Speak to God*
*Then Listen.*
Poetry taught me
To speak from the heart too
But to aim my reflections
In the opposite direction
To the Kingdom of Heaven
In the hearts of each of us.
She said;
*Give birth to words*
*That will walk*
*Amongst the outcasts*
*And the wounded*
*And the broken hearted.*
She paused
And I swear to God
It was as though
The universe paused with her;
*Cultivate words*
*That will provide respite*
*To those with sorrow*
*In their eyes*
*And stones in their hearts.*
*Your poems*
*Are how you serve*
*The living.*
I placed my hand over my heart
Bowed my head in reverence

Grateful for the words
I had been gifted
Put them in my basket
As provisions for the journey ahead.
Both prayer and poem
Emerge from the same centre
Flying like migrating birds
In different directions
Whose final destination
Is The One.

# Woman of God

A woman of God
Leaves remnants
Of the Sacred
In all the spaces
She graces.
Leaves traces
Of a fragrance
A whiff of which
Causes the seeker
To pursue The Source
That waters her garden.
Holy woman
In an *abaya* with Jordans
Or a maxi dress from Zara
Or a *Melfha* from Sahara.
Her presence brings comfort
No exchange of words necessary
No quoting of scripture necessary
No reciting of poetry necessary
She is of a kind
That reminds you
Of The Most High
Because her soul
Never left His Presence
When her mother gave birth
Bringing her glory to Earth.
Her heart bursts
All kinds of beauty
Whenever she hears the Name
Of her Beloved
On the tongue of saint
Or sinner
You see, she doesn't see forms
She sees the Maker of Forms
And the Knower of Hearts

Whose creation
Reminds her of flowers
Sprouting all around her.
She is like a Rose
In constant bloom
A perpetual full moon
Always in tune and present
In His Presence
Open to the unfolding
Of her Sweet Lord in every moment.
Handmaiden of the Most High
She whisper prayers into winds
And wakes whilst the world is sleeping
To speak with Him
The God of Abraham
The God of Moses
The God of Jesus
The God of Mary
The God of Muhammed ﷺ
She belongs to Him
And there is no Beauty in existence
For her, but Him
Her every act is a hymn
Her every move a sacred dance
She twirls like galaxies
For all who have eyes to see
She is one of God's greatest poems.
Her heart is a lamp
That hosts shards from His Light
Illuminating her face
And all who gaze upon it.
Beauty is a word
That can't hold her essence
But what other words do we have
To drape over her shoulders?
She leaves traces of the Sacred
In all the places she graces.

There are few things
In this world
More beautiful
Than a woman
who knows God.

# She Said

She said *Since God is with us*
*Shouldn't every moment be heavenly?*
He said *God is with us*
*Therefore every moment should be Godly*
*Heaven can't contain His Majesty.*
The difference was subtle.
But the distance as vast as the space
Between the seen and the unseen
A sharp reminder that her God
Concept was still incomplete.
She's still soaking in this process of gnosis
Still removing the robes of otherness
That she has carried on her back
For many lifetimes.
Waiting for Him
To secrete His Secret
Into her universe
Until there is no duality
Just The Reality
Just The One
*Ahadun Ahad.*
Before they shroud me
And lay my corpse toward the East
I seek to unlearn the fantasy
And taste the reality.
Remembering how to forget.
Dead before death.
Spirit before flesh.
God is all there was
And all that will be left.
God is all there *is*
And all that will be left.
And we think we're special
Even though our very existence
Is borrowed.

# World of Forms

What if this world of forms and all it contains were simply sign posts pointing us back to a God who is not limited by forms. Everything in this reality, manifest or hidden is pointing to the reality of God, right? In every moment there seems to be a message from Him just for me, just for you. He is never not in dialogue with His Creation, it's just that many of us have never been taught how to listen. Even when life delivers you a blow leaving a hole where your heart used to be, even when your flesh is on fire and tears cascade down your cheeks like a waterfall, all I see are opportunities for us to witness our fragility and learn to lean upon The Ever Living. Sometimes there's no point in fighting, sometimes the whole cosmos will be disrupted for Him to get your attention. Just surrender, Beloved, just surrender. If everything were perfect would we turn to Him empty-handed in the depths of night? How would we know light if we didn't experience darkness? How would we know joy if we didn't taste sorrow? How could we appreciate companionship if we didn't sit with solitude and how would we value life if we didn't witness the ruthlessness of death? All are signs posts pointing to the Majesty and Beauty of God. Being conscious of the Fingerprint of The Most High in every moment opens the possibility for us to dwell in the Abode of Eternal Nearness all the time. What a comforting thought.

# I Love You

I love you
Because I know
You hold within you
His greatest secret.
You just don't know it.
I only just found out.
The Breath of God in your essence
Is a doorway to His presence
And He is present, right now.
We are exactly where we are supposed to be.
Before our mothers wombs
Became midnight cocoons
For mortals with butterfly potential
To burst forth. Before
My spirit was dressed in flesh
Before His breath in Adam
Made Satan adamant
He not would bow
Before the vow
To deceive the sons of Adam
And his daughters
Before her waters broke
Before Jesus spoke
Before Abraham broke the idols
This moment was written.
Before I uttered the sentence
That was a return ticket to my essence
*Ashadu an lā ilāha illa -llāhu*
*Wa- ashadu anna muhammadan rasūlu-llāh*
Before I remembered my love for a man unlettered ﷺ
Who inhaled our maladies
And exhaled galaxies
For us to know God in all His Majesty
Whose face could make the sun set in shyness

And make the full moon become a crescent
Daring not to challenge his brightness
Before I was blinded
By his presence
This moment was written.
Before I married my reflection
Whose breath tastes of prayer
And remembrance
Before I loved him
And lost him
And found him again.
Heart opened, broken
And opened again.
Before my white gold wedding ring
Before I realised the black of his eyes
Resembled the pots of ink
That my destiny was written with
This moment was written.
Before Coltrane first blew
Before I knew what I knew
Before I didn't know
What I'll know tomorrow
Before the eventual sorrow
The comes from burying loved ones
And that bittersweet moment
When the tears subside
And you realise
The river of life
Just keeps flowing.
We are all notes in His Symphony
He is the Cause and the Cure
The before the before
And the after ever more.
Before that cold December morning
When God spoke through him, to me
And invited me on a journey

Over the hedges of make believe
Into the meadows of Reality.
*I Am Here, Right Here*
*Do You Not Want To Know Me?*
*I Was A Hidden Treasure*
*And I Wanted To Be Known*
*Do You Not Want To Know Me?*
As the frost settled on the ground
The purpose of my existence
Became clear as quartz crystal to me.
All signs pointed to *Rabbil Alameen*
Before the idols in my heart
Were smashed to smithereens
Before I realised the intricacies
Of the veils that imprison me
Before I learnt to seek
God's face in the city
And see His names manifest
In between breaths all around me.
*Ya Awwal Ya Akhir Ya Zahir Ya Baatin*
*Ya Awwal Ya Akhir Ya Zahir Ya Baatin*
*Ya Awwal Ya Akhir Ya Zahir Ya Baatin*
Before I dared to claim my existence
This moment was written.

# The Desert

My being yearns for the desert
For the stillness
The emptiness
The silence.
Drowning me out
Out of my mind
Drowning inside
Softly
Slowly
No me.
Face to face
With my naked nothingness
In the name of His Oneness
I bear witness
That we are less
Than dust
That dances
With wind
No us, just Him.
Lead me to a desert plane
Where nobody knows my name
And nobody cares
Busying their own hearts
With the sacred art
Of calling the Name
From which all life came.
Clad in 6 yards of fabric
Because the fact is
When my soul meets with eternity
I'll be shrouded this way.
Find me in the corner
Weeping like a mourner
Lamenting a lover.
Emptying my soul into the sand
Emptying my heart into His Hand

Until there are no bullets left in my chamber
Until I have no choice but to surrender;
*Do with me what you will Ya Rahman.*
I'm imagining a *Maghrib* sky
Where the heavens have rose-tinted cheeks
Like a virgin bride.
The scent of prayer
Perfuming the night
And when darkness arrives
We'll be cocooned in remembrance
And God's names will burst forth
From our lips
Like butterflies
To beautify
T h e    h o r i z o n.
I'm day dreaming
Of the desert's story
Because London's lights are blinding me
And I'm listening out for God's voice
But the city screams so loudly
I can't hear myself
Breathe.
I need some time away from a place
Where concrete competes
With my Lord's artistry
Every part of me
Is yearning for the Landscape
That Prophets would navigate
Cloaked only in God's Grace
Enchanted only by God's face
What I would do for a taste
Of how it feels to be erased
To be able to say
Sukina doesn't live here anymore
All that's left are God's Names

# The Fragrant Vagrant

Just the fragrance
Of those perfumed
By the Most Fragrant
Has turned me into a vagrant.
Forgotten what my name is
Or what I was doing
The moment
It happened.
Maybe I was sleeping.
Maybe I'm still dreaming
My heart is burning
And I can't put out these flames
Of Love.
My only aim is
To realise a love more ancient
Than the ancients,
A love that pulled me
From the depths of non-existence
When Allah was a Hidden Treasure
Alone in His Oneness.
My Lord said *Be* and it was
And there I was
And here we are.
I'm seeking a love
More sacred than the space
Where believers circumbulate
Or where the sinners pray
Or the wall where they wail
Or the bedroom chambers
Where mothers hold cupped hands
Up towards the heavens
Asking The Infinite to pour
His Grace upon us.
Pour Your Grace upon us
Until our cups runneth over

And love leaks through our fingers
Leaving a mess on the kitchen floor.
I'm seeking the reason they leave
Their homes in the first place.
Anticipating the taste
Of a love so sweet
They'll leave everything worldly
Everything temporal
To taste the Eternal.
I'm seeking the love
That makes the enraptured one
Stay gazing at the horizon
All the while gazing at His Face.
Witnessing His Unveilings
In every sway of the branches
Every fall of the leaves
Every rain drop, every cloud
Every breath and every breeze.
Just the fragrance
Of one perfumed
By the Most Fragrant
Has turned me into a vagrant
Inside is an ocean of insanity
Trying to hold myself together
And maintain my dignity
But most days
I think I might explode
Lumps of flesh and bone
Draped over the lamp post
From Love's overflow.
I have forgotten my name
And I don't know my way
Back home. In truth
I have no desire
To find my way
Back home
Ever again.

## 9

Walk
With
Women
Watered
With
Worship
Who
Witness the
Wonder and
Wounds
Within the
World
Who
Weep
Wearily
Whilst
Weaving
Wise
Words
Which
Will
Wake
Warriors
With
Wildflower
Wings to
Wade into the
Wilderness and
Write
Wisdom on
Walls.
Women
Wanderers
Who
Whisper

Wishes into
Wells
Who
Waltz
With the
Wax and the
Wane
Who
Water
Warm
Wombs
With
Worthiness
Waiting for
Wunderkind
*Walis* to
Wage
War on
Weak-heartedness.
Warriors
Without
Weapons
Who
Will
Walk on
Water
Without
Wings

# Invitation

One day Allah will invite me to His House
And I will be the happiest girl on Earth
And I'll cry for the whole of *Dhul Hijjah*
And then cry an ocean more.
Separation makes my heart sore
And my soul raw
And oceans pour
From tears ducts
That have no intention of drying up
Like seaways in the Sahara.
I yearn to make *tawwaf* around the *Ka'aba*
Like a human whirlwind in slow motion
Like the dance of the Milky Way
Like planets orbiting the sun
My soul yearns to orbit the Holy One
And devote my entire existence
Back into His Hand.
One day I'll visit *Masjid an Nabawi*
And greet the Jewel of Creation ﷺ
With the sweetest salutations
From a heart, cracked and broken
With palms wide open
With kohl on my fingertips
From wiping tears
Before the water cascades
Leaving a Tsunami on my face.
I yearn to bask under a *Madani* sun
And imagine I was one of his companions
Who lived in the time of revelation
When pieces of Heaven
Would descend to Earth
Settling in the pure heart chamber
Of God's Messenger ﷺ
My only desire to be near him

Sit in the corner
And absorb
The holy atmosphere
Of prophecy.
A glimpse of his face
Is all I am seeking
Eyes leaking
From the thought
That some day
I'll see him
And be under his gaze
And he will recognise
This flawed sinner
Bloated on ego
And wrongdoing -
Maybe he'll love me anyway.
One day my Lord will beckon me
To cross land and sea
To loose myself in the desert heat
And find myself
By following the fragrant breeze
Of *Nabi* Muhammed ﷺ
One day You will call
And I will come running
With my everything
With my nothing
Patiently awaiting
Your gracious invitation.

# Pray

Pray for Africa
And all of her children
Scattered across the globe
Like the Lost Tribes.
Pray for the African Americans
Slaughtered on street corners
By devils in blue suits.
Pray for Brazil
Pray for Congo
Pray for Darfur
Pray for Ethiopia
Pray for Eritrea
Pray for Grenfell
Pray for Haiti
Pray for Jamaica
Pray for Mali
Pray for Mozambique
Pray for Nigeria
Pray for 'Our Girls'
Pray for Palestine
Pray for Senegal
Pray for Somalia
Pray for Sudan
Pray for the rainforests
Pray for the oceans
Prayer for Mother Earth
Who cares for us all
So tenderly
By God's command.
Pray for the Native Americans
Pray for the Aborigines
Pray for the Indigenous tribes
Who know the language of the stars
And hear the lament of the trees.
Pray for the caretakers of Earth

Pray for the Children of Adam
Pray for the Children of Eve
Pray for Peace
Pray for humanity
And our heedlessness
And our lack of human-ness.
Pray for the enemy
That they be guided.
Pray for the victims
On both sides.
Pray for those who sleep
On streets and in subways
In Berlin
And Bristol
And Brussels
And Chicago
And London
And New York
And San Francisco
Pray for your community
Pray for your neighbourhood
And those suffering next door.
Pray for the poor
In money
And faith.
Pray for those who have no strength
To raise their hands to pray
To turn their face
To face the heavens
To face East
To speak
To God.
Pray for those whom
The world has made weary
For whom existence feels like a dull ache
In the pits of their stomachs
That they can't shake.

Pray for the Lost Ones
Who wish to be Found Ones.
Pray for the hungry
And thirsty
And homeless
And shoeless.
Pray for the addicts
Who can't kick the habit.
Pray for those you love
Pray for those you hate
Who make your heart
Twist with rage
And fill with flames
That no water can quell.
Pray for compassion
And mercy
And steadfastness
And patience.
Pray for the courage
To rest when necessary
And stand for justice
And speak truth to power
And fight when necessary
With your limbs
And your tongue
And your teeth
And your heart
And your whole soul.
Pray with your limbs
And your tongue
And your teeth
And your heart
And your whole soul.
Just pray, Beloved
Just pray.
Pray for yourselves

Pray for your life in this world
And your life in the world to come
After the universe has been folded up
And this world is a distant memory.
Pray for your mothers
And your fathers
And your children
Those you housed in your womb
And those you didn't.
Pray that our tomorrows
Be better than today
And that God's Peace
Descends rapidly
To cover us all.

'Prayer is the weapon of the believer.'

- Prophet Muhammed ﷺ

# I Wonder

I wonder what the world would be like if we left our egos at home and approached the world as though we were engaging with the Divine all of the time. Not him, her, they or them; just The One, in different disguises. How would we engage with each other? How would we witness the other? Would it make a difference to the way we listen, to the way we speak? What pieces of gold could we extract from every single interaction? What type of world could we create If we stopped seeing ourselves and the other and only saw expressions of His Oneness in every moment? What happens when we only seek God? Surely we would only see God, right? Sometimes I wonder.

# Divine Presence

Divine
Presence
Invite me in
I'll leave my shoes
At the bottom of the mountain
Walk towards the Burning Bush
Drowning.
Tell me a story
So I may share it
Your Mouth upon mine
Your Tongue
Because I have none.
Speak galaxies
Through me.
Speak life
Into existence
Within me
Let me give birth
To the words
That you want
To be heard
Down here on Earth.
Swimming in the air
Dancing on water
Praying upon a fire
That can't burn me
Because there is no me.
O Holy of Holies
Grant me an eternity
In Your Proximity.

# Love and Longing

May I use this moment
To speak from a heart
That's still beating but broken
Unsure if this is prayer or poem
But I'll keep going.
Wounds that can never be healed
Are now showing
In my eyes, there's a pain
That can't be disguised
But I keep going
Knowing
That even if I never gaze
Upon the subject of my longing
The fact that I know His name in the first place
Means I'm already grazing in His Grace.
My heart's inclining
Feels like it's climbing
Out of my torso
Into that portal
Between God and mortal
So I may know what Adam's fall was for.
Not sure, when it became normal
For me to stand at bus stops
Waiting for the veil to drop
Aching for the illusion to stop
Not sure when it became normal
For me to desperately
Yearn for Him to turn to me
Well pleased for the rest of eternity,
This distance is burning me.
Understand when I speak
It's not secrets I seek
Not miracles or mysteries
I just want my existence to be

In line with a time before history
A time before time
Before the first moment passed
When we grasped
With our entire being
What we were seeing
Witnessing Him
With our everything.
Our purpose a Hymn
Praising Him
I'm craving Him
Like a fiend of the sweetest decree
No other love can satisfy me.
Oh sweet memory
Don't fail me now
I know He is near
But don't know how
To tell Him
I love Him
Can't stop thinking of Him
Will never cease seeking Him
Until my last breath exits my body
Like the fragrant smoke
From a stick of incense
Or a bundle of sage
Or Cambodian *Oud* resting on charcoal.
I tread these streets calling His name
Riding trains seeking His Face
Even in the darkest places
Where the people seem so far away
Pain smothered across their faces
Because they've forgotten the way
Were never told there's another way
To do this life thing.
I pray for His Grace
To descend like summer rain
Or even a Hurricane

I just want to feel His Nearness
Pelting against my window pane.
What do I do with a heart covered in flames?
Ya Allah! You know why I came
And why I remain chained to those
Who call to Your Way.
The seasons are starting to change
I can feel it in the air
London's winter is drawing near
Where smiles between strangers are rare
But I'm still singing the songs of the lovers
As if it were summer
And I strive to remember
That God is the Giver
And I ask that He give me Him.
I strive to remember
Until I forget
Everything but Him.
Awaiting my turn
Expecting nothing in return
Waiting for Him to whisper my name
And invite me home once again.

Listen to a recording
of this poem here

# If Only You Knew

God didn't bring your essence
Out of non-existence
For no reason.
You were not designed
To dwell in insignificance
You are not an accident
You are no coincidence.
Your excellence
Painted the heavens
With a masterpiece so unique
The stars, the moon, the cosmos
Lost the ability to speak
And they are still silent
In awe of God's Craft
His Breath in our torso
Our souls are eternal
Our imagination a portal
To a land beyond the rainbow.
We are more brilliant than we
Could ever imagine
Galaxies dance beneath our skin
Beloved, let that sink in.
The biggest myth that exists
Is that we are merely mortal
That we were meant to be normal
And conform to norms
That don't have our names on it.
Let me just say this;
God's greatest secret
Is closer to you
Than you are to your own self
You are the holiest temple, Beloved.
Maybe you were never told
But now you know

Never allow anyone to reduce you
To flesh and blood and bones.
Let your soul unfold
Let it stretch towards the sun
Let your existence be
A continual manifestation
Of the Beauty
Of the One.

# Soft

I have a soft spot
For soft hearts
Those with soft cheeks
Watered by warm tears
Who speak soft words
Into warm ears.
Who wear soft scarves
Framing their soft face
Who put their soft heads
On prayer rugs
When they pray.
Who walk softly
And sleep lightly
And love deeply
And cry frequently
From the tender love
They have for their Lord.


*(Dedicated to Sabah and Hafsa)*

# What The Moon Taught Me

Whilst driving down the motorway at nightfall, I noticed a beautiful full moon emerge from behind the dark clouds. It looked as though the moon was unveiling herself, sharing her beauty with those on Earth, allowing us to catch a glimpse of her celestial beauty. I was in awe, captivated by the majesty of the moon. There were moments when the moon was so bright it felt as though there was nothing in existence but me and her. Other times the moon was covered by clouds granting me an occasional glimpse from behind a veil. At one point I couldn't see the moon at all. I was searching for her face only to realise that the moon was behind us all along. I couldn't always see the moon but she was always present. This became a personal message to me, reminding me of my relationship with God. Sometimes I feel so close to Allah it's as though there is nothing in existence but Him. In His unfathomable generosity He allows me to draw near and bask for a moment or two in His Presence. Other times it feels as though there are veils made of iron and concrete between me and my Maker. Sometimes the distance feels so permanent I wonder if I will ever get a chance to taste the nearness I crave. Like the clouds, these veils of life can give the illusion that God is distant, but after a while He reveals Himself and I feel ashamed for ever doubting His nearness. *Fa Inni Qareeb* 'Indeed I am near,' God told us, on the tongue of His Messenger ﷺ. Just like when I couldn't see the moon only to realise it was actually behind us lighting our path home all along, Allah is always present, closer to us than our own selves. Even in our darkest moments when we feel far away from our Creator, may we always remember that He is always there. Why would He ever leave you Beloved?

## Company of Lovers

After the final pint has been pulled,
And the pub doors are shut tight
After the last nightclub has spat the last reveller
Out onto the cold pavement
When the streets are silent
And the last cab driver has delivered
The last after-work drinker to safety
When the early morning frost has started to settle
On grass blades and window panes
Coating the sleepy city in silver
There is a living room
In North West London
With the light on.
Nestled between a railway and a children's playground
Freight trains sing freedom songs in the background
And if you look close enough
You'll see God's lovers, huddled
On the floor
On chairs
Half asleep
Hearts awake
Still singing His praise.
Loud enough for their hearts to hear
But low enough for the neighbours to dream
Uninterrupted of brighter tomorrows.
How many ways can we say *La Illaha Illallah*
How many melodies can we make to testify to His Oneness.
How long until we see His Oneness
Until His Oneness becomes us
And we leave our otherness
At the bottom of the stairs
With our shoes.
Drunken smiles and giddy merriment
Beautified praise has made us tipsy
Without the stench of liqueur

Clinging to our teeth.
Each breath is a love song to God.
Each mention of His Name
Causes Eternity
To be etched into our DNA.
Each utterance of His name
Causes the universe to slip away
Eyes closed we sit, we smile, we sway
Located in a time outside of time
And a place beyond space.
I could never underestimate
The grace that emanates
From keeping company with lovers
In pursuit of God's Face.
Every tongue tattooed with His Names
Every single heart aflame
All gathered to splatter His Praise
Across urban landscapes.

*(Dedicated to the Fetugas)*

How can you expect to experience
His Love when you don't roll
With those who love Him?
Unashamedly.
Hearts on Fire
Burning all desires
For other than Him.
Join the company of Lovers
And ride the Caravan to His Presence
Right now beloved,
What are you waiting for?

# Saints in the City

This is not a Poem
More of a dedication
To the patient ones
Who seek God's Face in the city.
Those who wake to catch the sun rise
Even if only into grey skies
Because it reminds them of the Majesty of their Lord.
Those who seek the sun's decline behind
Graffiti patterned railway lines
Praying for orange and red light
To paint blast the sky
Because they realise
If you look close enough
God always sends us signs.
Even when street lamps dull the stars in the sky
They try. Even though high rise buildings
Barricade the skyline. They try.
We are not the ones with desert nights
Where the full moon gives enough light
To read scriptures by bedsides.
We are the ones who can't make it out
To sacred lands to sit at the feet
Of the enlightened, who teach
The mysteries of Allah
With the subtleties of silence
Whose very fragrance is guidance
For the now guided seeker
Who sleeps in sacred lands
That are watered by *Quran*
And prayerful utterances
By those who can transform
Sinners into Saints.
Places that taste like heaven
Make London feel like a nightmare
She'd rather forget.

No street fights, no police sirens
No force-ripe children
No people trying to earn a living
On broken pavements to pay rent.
This is for those who seek *Mustapha*
The Chosen One ﷺ
In the land of the frozen sun
Where we need machines
That blow heat to help us sleep
But each chilly night here
There are those who dream
Of the unseen and catch of a gleam
Of His Reality.
Waking up in tower blocks
With unwavering conviction
That there is a God.
This is an ode to those who seek
Allah in the city
Looking for light in a land
Of dark days and dark nights
Tense hearts and bitter minds.
To those who still seek the light in people's eyes
Because they know with certainty
That we are all a manifestation of God's signs
And everyone is reaching for Him
Even if they don't realise.
This is for those with mercy in their eyes
Whose prayers have the power to pierce the skies
Irregardless of where you reside
God always hears His servants' cries.
To those who ride the train
Reading sacred scrolls
From masters of the soul
Causing their hearts to explode
And come back together
Between Oxford Street and Tottenham Court Road
They cause the carriage to glow

And nobody would know
That columns of Angels
Follow them wherever they go.
There are saints in our city, didn't you know?
Friends of Allah, walking down the High Road.
To those who clutch prayer beads tight
Their intimate companion in the depths of the night
As each bead passes through fingertips
His most Beautiful Names stain their lips.
And they send prayers on the Prophet ﷺ
Until they no longer exist
Their bodies exist in this metropolis
But their souls have found bliss.
They know the whole earth is a *Masjid*
So make sacred spaces wherever they see fit
Illuminating pavements with worship
They lay down prayer mats
Behind buildings that scrape the sky
Because Allah deserves to be praised
Any time, any place. Blessed is His Name.
To those who seek knowledge of the Sacred
So learn from virtual sages
Add Sudanese *Qaris* to Spotify playlists
Seeking ways to satisfy their cravings
For nearness to God, in the city.
To those who have come to the conclusion
That this whole world is an illusion
That will one day fade
And all that will be left is His Face.
To those who seek God's Grace
In the city
To you I dedicate this.

*(Dedicated to Shaykh Babikir
and the people Rumi's Cave)*

Listen to a recording
of this poem here

Watch a video
of this poem here

47

# I Am That, I Am

Sometimes I find myself
Looking up to the heavens
To the celestial bodies
The glowing moon
The blazing stars
To find myself.
Or across the vast Earth
The endless oceans
The crowded cities
To catch a glimpse of my truth.
Seeking pieces of myself
Scattered across the cosmos
Sprinkled upon the unseen.
Until my heart reminded me
That I am what I am looking for.
I am, that I am.
I am whole
And perfect
Not splintered
Nor incomplete
Or ill-prepared for the journey ahead.
Why constantly look outside
To find the Reality of Existence
The secret of which, exists inside
This fleshy temple, and beyond.
Who am I searching for
That doesn't live closer to me
Than my own hand upon my own heart?
Whose melody is more beautiful
Than the one emanating from my tongue?
Whose face am I constantly
Searching for my features upon?
Who can lead me to completion
That isn't with me all along?
Nobody can tell my story

Sing my hymns
Heal this heart
Love me entirely
Pen this poetry
This beautiful poetry
But me.
God has given me
All the tools I need
For my short time
Here on Earth.
I am
What I
Have been
Seeking
All along.
What a blessing
It is, to come home
To myself.
Finally.

# Secret

Sometimes
Those with the deepest secret
Speak the softest
Or barely speak at all.
Their gaze can shift you.
Their state can lift you
From bus stops and subways
Into the darkness of space
Into the light from His Face
Into the presence of His Grace
Into nothingness.
Into Oneness.
All the while
No words have been uttered.
Sometimes those with the
Realest secret
Have become their secret
No need to speak
To secrete it
Those who truly seek it
Will find it
Intertwined in the space
Between their lines.
Sometimes those with
The Most beautiful secret
Barely say a word.

# His Voice Sounds Like Medina

His voice sounds like Medina al Munawarra
Illumination clings to his every word.
I can see it with my heart
I can feel it from afar.
Last night my chest was pierced
By Muhammadan lights
Through my *Shaykh al Murabbi*
Who is in the city of my *Nabi* ﷺ
Ya Ahmed ﷺ
Ya Mahmood ﷺ
This love is contagious
And how could it not be?
He is heartbeats away
From *Masjid an-Nabawi.*
A green dome crowns the final home
Of he who made my Lord known to me.
Ya *Habibullah* ﷺ
Ya *Rasullulah* ﷺ
I close my eyes I am there
Lost in the Prophet's Mosque
With no desire to be found
By anyone other than him.
Oh how I wish I was an *Ansari*
Awaiting the arrival of this Noble *Hashimi* ﷺ
Grazing the edge of the city
Gazing into eternity.
Oh how I wish it was me
That first saw God's beloved ﷺ
And Abu Bakr as-Siddiq
Illuminating the horizon.
I wish I had sung with the women
*Jita Sharraftal Madina*
*Marhaban yā khayra dā*
I can smell the Musk of *Madinat un Nabi*
When he talks to me

I can feel the breeze from *Jannat al Baqi*
When he prays for me.
And in that moment
I was certainly not in London.
I was basking in an earthly / heavenly garden
My tears seeping into the carpet
My heart seeking my Beloved.
His prayers sound different from Medina
As though his vocal chords
Are encased with more grace.
I imagine even more *Noor* decorates his face
Reflecting the secret of the Prophet
Resting in that place.
*Nabi ar-Rahma.*
*Mustafa.*
*Taha.*

ﷺ

And from this Blessed City
He answers a call from me
His poverty-stricken mureedah
Continents away, calling just to say
*Salaam Alayka Shaykh Mahy*
*How is Medina, Ya Sayyidi?*
I can hear the love in his heart
When he tells me how beautiful it is
In this courtyard of his beloved ﷺ
By Allah, I can feel it.
And some of that love
Has found its way
Into my blistered heart
And heals it.
The moon is glowing
On this *Ramadan* evening
And some lovers of God
Are huddled around one telephone
Speaking in gentle tones

As though we were sitting with him
Under a lavender sky in Medina
The land that gave Solace
To the final Prophet ﷺ
*Shaykh, please greet the Prophet for me*
*In your prayers Ya Shaykh*
*Please remember me*
*He is my gate*
*And you are my means*
*And I am in need.*
He sends a symphony of prayers my way
Every single word pierced me like a light ray
*May the love of the Prophet ﷺ fill your heart*
*May the love of Allah fill your heart*
*May you know the Secrets of Allah*
*And may Allah Love you.*
I never knew Medina had a love song
That clings to the throats of its lovers
But yesterday I heard it
In the voice of my Shaykh.
And I swear to God
It intoxicated my soul.


*(Dedicated to my guide, Shaykh Mouhamadou Mahy Cissé)*

Listen to a recording
of this poem here

# A Mureedah's Prayer

May we inherit from the inheritors
And benefit from the benefactors
And be loved by the lovers.
And be prayed for
By the people of prayer
Be guided by pure guides
Be near to those drawn near
And serve those who serve.
May we give to those who give
And be increased by those increased
And receive from those who have received.
May we be present with those who are
present
In The Holy Presence in every state.
May we follow those who follow
In the footsteps of the Messenger ﷺ
As best they can and never waver.
May we gaze into the eyes of those
Who have gazed into the eyes of those
Who have gazed into the eyes
Of the Beloved ﷺ
May we be loved by those
Who are loved by Him
And never leave their side
Not for the world and all it contains.
May we inherit from the inheritors.

Ameen.

# The Angel & The Trumpet

There is an Angel standing
Lips to a trumpet
Light years long
Waiting for Allah's word
To blow.
Made for no other purpose
Than to play in that moment
A song so devastatingly beautiful
All the living will fall out of existence
And taste death.
In one breath
All that will be left
Is the Face of your Lord.
And the Universe will be silent
Imagine the sound
of the
Universe
Silent.
Holy
   Golden
      Silence.
And God will be alone is His Oneness
As He was in the beginning
And as He shall be in the end
And as He's always been.

# Lessons in Letting Go and Letting God

Hold in high esteem those who have hurt you, Beloved. You don't have to understand their actions, you don't have to like their motives but when you choose to surrender to the reality of the situation and accept this unfolding as part of Divine Order a door is opened for you to flee to God for solace. He is waiting for you there. When your heart is shattered, when your limbs are bleeding and the light from your soul is leaking onto the pavement, flee to Him, I promise you He is waiting to comfort and restore you. Seek out His Company and make Him your Sanctuary. Draw near to the Holy One, Beloved, draw near. A time will come when you will be able to forgive those who hurt you because you get it now, they were a chapter in your dazzling life story and you'll thank them for the lessons in darkness because it taught you how to harvest your own light. Their actions taught you that God is the goal. They taught you to flee to the Presence of the Eternal Friend. What mercy they carried in their palms disguised of darkness. What a gift. Someday soon you will reach a point when you will think of them and you will see them bathed in God's Grace. Light and forgiveness will flow from your heart to theirs like pure water. No pain, just love. We are all lessons for each other, envelopes from God with invitations inside, admission tickets for entrance to the Courtyard of His Presence. Every atom in existence is manifesting God's Will, following Divine Orders and when we understand this, this becomes a pathway to spiritual growth and healing. May we be from amongst those who witness Him with every breath and make Him our Perfumed Refuge in times of pain and in times of ecstasy. The Divine Doors are wide open Beloved. May we enter and never leave.

# Lover's Tongue

The spark of Creation
Must have been
The sweetest
Love song
Ever.
The melody of which
Caused universes
To burst forth from nothingness
And exist in a state of bliss
Can you imagine this?
*Be* He said; in a tongue
So ancient and sacred
So fragrant and laden
With love.
I guess love
Must have sounded
Like that moment
Because in that moment
Love is all there was
And still, love is all that is.
Each dawn, birds in tribes
Spread wings and sing
To usher in new light
Painting the sky
With songs the colour of love
And longing. The way our hearts
Would sound if they escaped
Our chests and took flight.
One glorious night
The moon spoke to me
In a tongue so sweet
She said;
*His Love is always present*
*Although your eyes can't see*
*Just as I am always full*

*Even if a crescent is all you see.*
Believe me
The universe
Is the most eloquent narrator
If only we took the time
We could have the most delicious
Dialogue with The Divine
As He sings through His Signs
What else is a crimson sunset
But a poem in the sky?

Remembrance
of God is
sweeter
than honey.

## Make *Dhikr*

Make Dhikr until there is no you left
Until you have no breath left
Until you have no time left
To do anything but make Dhikr.
Make Dhikr with every breath
Make Dhikr make you breathless
Until your mind becomes lifeless
Quiet, silenced.
Maybe then you'll be able to hear
A voice that is timeless.
Heart Speak.
Truth so sweet
From a place inside
Where my Lord resides
Make Dhikr to polish His Throne
Make Dhikr and let Him be known
Make Dhikr flow from your tongue's tip
Like melodies from an Angel's trumpet
Make Dhikr till you have parched lips
That no water can quench
Make Dhikr until you feel
Heaven's kiss ever-so gently
Whisper remembrance aplenty
Make Dhikr when your heart's full
And when you feel
Hollow
Broken
Empty.
Let Dhikr mend you
Let Angels commend you
Make Dhikr in Multitudes or in Solitude.
Make Dhikr in times of gratitude.
And when you don't understand
What God is doing with you
Just Make Dhikr

Make Dhikr until you feel
Your heart exhale in gratitude.
Make Dhikr to drown the *Nafs*
Immerse your ego's head
In an ocean of *Asma ul Husna*
Salawat un *Nabi* ﷺ
And *La ilaha il Allah*
Make Dhikr like your life depends upon it
Because the life of your spirit depends upon it.
Make Dhikr like there is no tomorrow
Because there is no tomorrow
The only Truth is this moment
So Remember your Lord
Until your heart is blown open
Until your soul is awoken
Until your lips are in motion
Even when your eyes are closed.
Make Dhikr
Until the Dhikr becomes you
Until there is no distance
Between the Name and the Named
Make Dhikr because Allah said:
*Remember Me and I'll Remember you*
Make Dhikr until you realise
There is no you
Just Him.
Remembering
Himself
Upon
Your sweet lips.

# The Many Faces of Love

### I.

The topic today is love.
We are talking about painful love
That shameful love
The lost all your dignity on the pavement love
It's the same for us. We go insane for love.
I'm talking about a heart being devoured by love
Like a mother being eaten by her own child type love
The derangement, enslavement, heart in flames type love
Like a vagabond on the open road
This type of love will kill you in your own home
And no-one will ever know.
Never suspect the cause of your demise
Is the very same love you sought all your life
For love, you have given your life
The topic today is love.


### II.

Love can make the sane walk out the front door
And wake up on psychiatric wards
Having forgotten their own names
And from where they came.
Love can make the mildest amongst us
Lay awake at night plotting the demise
Of the one who stole her love
Leaving a raging hole
Where her heart used to be
*She used to be so sweet* they said
*I can't believe she watched him bleed to death.*
Love can make you leave your desk,
Step out of your office
Walk down the stairs
Breathe in the afternoon air

Start running and running
And never look back
Destination: anywhere closer to love.

### III.
Love makes lovers leap off mountain peaks
Hands clasped like iron casts.
One last kiss before they glide
Through the air like spring blossoms
I wonder if time slows down for them
In those final moments
Before their bodies crack against the ocean's limbs.
If they can't be together life itself is undesirable.
The fragrance of Jasmine flowers
The innocent smile of a child
The taste of honey, contains no charm
The Earth itself becomes a prison yard
For the one separated from love.

### IV.
Love is a desert woman
Sitting in embroidered tents
Begging the spirit of the sand
To return her beloved man
She has been seeking behind every sunset
Since he left with the caravan.
Gazing into tomorrow
Face cupped in the palm of her henna'ed hands
Her beauty disguises her violently
Beating, bleeding heart.
Outside she's a work of art
Inside she's falling apart
Love makes her spend a moment longer
With her face in the sand
Uttering prayers whilst kissing God's Hand
Breath and tears form litanies that she hopes
Will be caught by Angels and flown to God's Throne

Maybe He'll hear her
Maybe then, she'll no longer be alone

## V.

Love is the way Coltrane kissed his saxophone
In that moment you would think they were all alone
No band, no audience, no stage, no microphone
Just the Player and the Played in a dreamy haze
Then he awakes and realises, everyone
Was watching them
Make love.
Love can make the universe fall out of existence
Love can make him want to gift her all of existence
Name stars after her
Etch her name into trees
Offer her the galaxy
As though the whole cosmos
Was part of his inheritance.

## VI.

Love is Rumi and Shams at-Tabriz locked away
Love is the jealousy his students felt
When they saw *Maulana* drifting
From this temporal world of forms and decay.
Unaware this preparation for his annihilation
Meant he would have to set fire to his reputation
Set fire to his idols and set fire to himself
He had to die in the name of Love
To be resurrected in the name of Love.
Shams and Rumi; divine love embodied
Dipped their toes into infinity
Whilst sipping on Eternity
Nothing in existence to either
But student and teacher
Until there was neither
Just ether

And the Supreme Being; Love.
When his love was ripped from him
Rumi dipped his pen into his soul
And wrote volumes of gold.
Love made Rabia al Adawiyya the saint
Walk through the streets with water and flames
To quench hell's fire and set paradise aflame
*I do this Only For His Face* she said
*I worship Only For His Face.*
Not for paradise gardens, rivers of honey or lakes
Heaven for me is to gaze upon God's Face.

VII.

Love
Pulled me through the sky
To catch a glimpse
Of my beloved's face
Not for the sake of his face
You understand that, right?
But for the sake of the One
Who created his face.
To graze under the gaze
Of one who knows the way
His remembrance of God
Made me lose myself
His presence in His Presence
Made me forget my name
Set my heart on fire
Outside I look the same
But inside I'm a woman deranged
Trying to put out these flames of love.
Did I mention that love is insane!
And there is no-one to blame but myself
Whoever told me to follow
Love's blazing trail

Forgot to tell me
That I would lose myself
Prayed *Salatul Janaza*
Over my temporary shell
The part of me that is make-believe
I watched my old carcass drift out to sea
Feeling afraid and free
At exactly the same time.
Most days I'm walking
But inside I'm drowning
My eyes leak to let the water out
Leaving oceans on carpets
Separation is the hardest
Until you remember you can't
Be separated from yourself.
Love causes the lover to disappear.
In a puff of smoke
Until all that's left
Is a discarded cloak
Burnt at the edges
Where I used to be.
Love laughs
Watching us attempt
To follow her way
*You have no idea*
She laughs
*You really have*
*No idea.*

66

God bless those whose hearts are soft as *Zam Zam* water
Whose eyes flood at the mention of His name
Who wipe tears from faces
With Hijabs or fingertips
Wanting no-one around to notice
Their love for the Beloved ﷺ
Has taken over.

# Gratitude, Always.

We give thanks for our broken hearts
Because only in the castle's ruins
Can the treasure be found.
We kiss the hands of the one
Whose sledgehammer
Smashed our hearts into shards
Because only in our brokenness
Can God gather the pieces
And put back us together
Even more perfectly than before.
When our spirit is being tested
And our heart is being stretched
Wide across the horizon
And our bodies are being pushed
Way beyond its limits
Hold tight, Beloved
God is emptying you out
So He can fill you to the brim
With Him. *Al Hamdullilah.*
The Beauty is imminent
And God is ever-so close.

# Lord of the Pen

Lord of the Pen
And of men
And their daughters
Their seeds and of water
Of laughter and order
Of breast milk and slaughter
Lord of the Light and of twilight
Death and spring
The First and the Last
The Beginner of things
Lord of the mountain tops
The tower blocks
The gliding birds
The universe
And its expansion
Lord of the Heavenly hosts
And the Heavenly mansions
Lord of Mars and of Saturn
Of stellar patterns
That dot the sky like Aboriginal art
You opened my heart just as little
And since then I've become a vagrant
Just from the fragrance of Your friends.
I yearn one day
To have a heart so cleansed
His Throne resides therein.
Imagine when this world
Becomes a distant lullaby
Some will be able to see their Lord
Like a full moon on a crisp winters night.
O my Lord
How can I love you more
How can I make this jaw
So in awe
That each movement
Makes music to glorify my Lord.

Lord of the veils of separation
Lord of light's manifestation
Lord of patience.
Each inhalation
Is by Your Command
Every secret of the sea
Every legend of the land
In Your Hand.
I am floored by the invitation
To love You more
I mean, You own the draw
That pulled me to Your Door in the first place
This world of forms is starting to fade
And my only desire is Your Face
So with these fingers made of clay
I'm trying to convey
My heart's tongue upon this page
As reminders of these first days
Whilst my words are still sane
Because tomorrow may not be the same.
I contemplate on my wonder years
And my yesterdays
When I sought solace in the seen
And eternal happiness in human beings
Now I've awoken from a dream within a dream
To a *Deen* within a Deen
Where my only purpose for being
Is seeking The Supreme.
My Lord is turning me inside out
Breaking my idols
Breaking me down
So now, when I put my face to the ground
I mean it. And when I lift my hands to the heavens
I mean it. Cup empty, please fill it
And over spill from it
Beyond this pen

Beyond these lyrics
Beyond the world of men
And the world of spirits
May these words exist
Like the Northern Lights
Beautiful fleeting moments in time
All pointing toward The Divine
Lord of the Pen
Lord of mankind.

If the people you roll with don't have love cascading from their eyelids, seeping from every pore of their bodies, dripping from their lips like honey, crashing from their tongues like the waves of a holy ocean against the shore of your being; if the people you roll with don't make you fall in love, or love love, or love yourself or love God, I'm sorry to say this Beloved, but you may need to find some new companions.

# Wake Up

Wake beloved
Whilst the city sleeps
And souls are resting
Recovering from the weariness
Of the world and the thickness
Of this *Dunya*. Wake up
Whilst limbs lay horizontal
And the body has started
To heal flesh and mend bones.
Wake when the sun caresses
Another part of the Earth.
Climb gently out of your bed
Whisper His Holy Name over water
And anoint your face
Limbs and crown.
Dim the lights
Light a candle
Or a lamp that leaks
A nostalgic glow.
Dress in soft garments
That sit gently on your skin
And make you feel holy
Perfume your sanctuary
With the type of fragrances
That invite angels to gather
In your garden of devotion
And pray alongside you
Or observe you
You, sweet child of Adam
Sweet daughter of Eve
Grazing in God's Meadow.
Lay your prayer mat down
Face the East
And come to God
He is waiting for you there

With Palms wide open
To receive your heavy load.
Pour your prayers upon the carpet
Cover the walls with longing
Douse your chamber with tears
And set the room ablaze
With praise.
Wake up beloved
When the moon is the host in the heavens
And the stars have laid a banquet in the sky
A gift for the eyes
Of all who care to look up
At a time when most souls
Are drifting in and out of dream states.
Give Him all of you
You don't need to say a word
You can just sit there
He knows your heart
And the weight it holds
And your wounds left open
Let Him heal them for you.
Make Him your companion
When darkness curtains the heavens
Wake in the depths of the night
When the breeze is but a whisper
And the trees are deep in slumber
When bonfires are now embers
And the Friends of God gather
Like a constellation of candles
Under the velvety sky
To remember and draw near
To The Most Near
To The Most High.
Wake up, Beloved
Wake up.

# The Bringer of the Divine Flood

You gave me an appetite for annihilation
Taught me to leave my ego
At the bottom of the stairs and come
Taught me everything in this *dunya* is fading
Except the One
Even my existence
So leave that too and come.
You taught me the wealth of having nothing
And the poverty in having everything.
You made me forget my own name
Then taught me my Real Name
Taught to seek God's Face
On the Horizon and within myself.
Now I know myself
And speak from a tongue
That makes no empty claims
A tongue that talks only from taste
And I've never even seen your face
Ya *Barhama*.
Niasse.
You taught me to love
*Sayyidina* Muhammed 🕌
In the way that is deserved
Taught me to seek his light
Until my eyes started burning
Until my heart started glowing
Tears flowing from your ocean
Back into your ocean
*Minka Ilayka*
This is more than a poem.
Cheeks wet
Bated breath
Chest split open
Heart exploded
Broken into a million pieces
And a million more

Stitched back together with the Litany
Of Shaykh Ahmed al Tijani
That you gifted me
This *Dhikr* blew life into me
*Salatul Fatihi* blew light into me
You gave me the ability
To yearn for *Nabi* Muhammed ﷺ
Like a beggar with nothing left
The epitome of emptiness
My only desire to be counted
Amongst the beloved's beloveds.
My only desire to be filled with Ahmed ﷺ.
My soul lives on the steps
Where your blessed body rests
*Salatul Fatihi* perfuming my breath
My tears in the soft carpet
My heart no longer dead.
Because somebody said:
Leave the warmth of your bed
Go to *Kaolack* instead
Ask for Shaykh Ibrahim Niasse
You won't be disappointed
There you will find cupbearers
Serving Knowledge of God
From a well overflowing
His followers have drowned in Dhikr
Their faces are glowing
It's like *Baye Niasse* has a Divine Ocean
Leaking from his fingertips
Even a few droplets
Can make you intoxicated
Remembrance that will leave you enraptured
Lost in God the Most Beautiful Captor.
So I came seeking, heart bleeding
Knowing nothing in existence is more pressing
Than this invitation to God's Presence.

We came wounded and broken
Burning spirits and hearts split open
Riding taxis like chariots of fire
Upon dusty roads
To drown in your watering hole
With aspirations of becoming whole.
The legend about you is true
What the Mauritanian poets penned
About you is true
You came with more than we knew
And maybe we'll never know
The depth of your secret
But still we keep reaching
For the station we're seeking
Nearness to God
Until He is all we are seeing
Nearness to God
Until He is all we are being
With the light of Muhammed ﷺ
As our beacon.

*Dedicated to Shaykh Ibrahim Niasse*

# Salatul Fatihi

اَللَّهُمَّ صَلِّ عَلَى سَيِّدِنَا مُحَمَّدٍ اَلْفَاتِحِ لِمَا أُغْلِقَ وَ اَلْخَاتِمِ لِمَا سَبَقَ نَاصِرِ الْحَقِّ
بِالْحَقِّ وَ الْهَادِي إِلَى صِرَاطِكَ الْمُسْتَقِيمِ وَ عَلَى آلِهِ حَقَّ قَدْرِهِ وَ مِقْدَارِهِ الْعَظِيمِ

O Allah, bless our Master Muhammed, who opened what was
closed and sealed what was before. He makes the truth victorious by
the truth and he is the guide to Your Straight Path. And bless his
Household as it befits his immense stature and splendour
.

Allahumma salli 'alā Sayyidinā Muhammadini l-Fātihi limā ughliq,
wa l-khātimi limā sabaq, nāsiri l-haqqi bi l-haqq, wa l-hādī ilā
sirātika l-mustaqīm, wa 'alā ālihi haqqa qadrihi wa miqdārihi l-'azīm.

# The Contradiction of Existence

I am a manifestation of Magnificence
Created by The Master Sculptor
Who blew Himself into me.
I am more cosmic than the cosmos
Galaxies exist beneath my eyelids
I hold universes in my torso
And oceans in my bloodstream
The sun sets in my chest
I am the east and the west
Life and death
At exactly the same time.
I am *gifted* and *self-hatred*
Dancing under the moonlight.
I am loved and lonely
Afraid and courageous
Safe and dangerous
Laughing and crying
Slipping and flying
Through this experience
That we call life.
I am forever and never
Swaying back and forth
Through time and space.
I am an expression
Of His Oneness
Even if the fallacy of duality
Is what my tongue proclaims.
The myth that I exist
Makes me giggle sometimes.
I am inside every particle
That illuminates existence
I am eternity enveloped in a mortal
Human beings
Are we not wonderful?

# The Journey Home

One thing I've come to know with all my heart, is that we are all desperately trying to find our way home. No matter how many veils we may wrap up in to protect ourselves from having to face the Truth, the truth is, beyond the noise and clutter of life the voice of the soul never stops asking for you to follow the road that will take you back home. Some are born with guidance as their birthright like a golden spoon in their mouths, the only thing they have to do is put one foot in front of the other and walk the path carved out by their forefathers and mothers. All they have to do is press play and let the music unfold into a beautiful melody. Others don't have such clarity; some are born into darkness like a secret hidden under the stairs. But every now and then a Light from a distant galaxy invites them to play with Angels who sing songs of praise under the moonlight. A conversation ensues between this Light and the secret in their souls but they don't understand it yet. The road is long and life itself is the guide that will teach them. Sometimes whilst the world sleeps they cry into pillows and if a loved one lying next to them asks them what the cause is of their sorrow, they gaze into the darkness but have no words. How do you describe a deep longing from beyond your heart for a Truth older than the sun? They know there is something more but where does one begin their pursuit? In which direction do they point their compass? And sometimes when life is too dense and they can't find the magic beyond the concrete they seek a way out, inhaling herbs wrapped in paper in hopes that they may float with the smoke to the other side of the rainbow, only to wake up the following morning veiled and aching even more. These people are known as dreamers, rebels or outcasts. They are often misunderstood because they walk to a different rhythm. They tend to be artistic because the light they carry is constantly seeking the horizon and if they don't get it out it feels as though they might just explode, right there on the pavement leaving only a trace of stardust. They outgrow the small towns from whence they came, arriving in big cities with a backpack full of dreams and a sparkle in their eyes reflecting the Light from that distant galaxy we spoke about earlier. Sometimes they are illuminated and other times degraded, sometimes it seems as though they are knocking on heaven's gates, other times they wake in the gutter with dirt on their face. It's just like that sometimes. But they will be the first in the squad to notice the rainbows in the sky on a damp London afternoon or point out Orion's Belt when the heavens turn a navy shade of blue. These seekers are my favourite kind, because they've lost blood and teeth, lost friends and parts of themselves to eventually find within themselves the treasure they were longing for all along. These brave-hearted wayfarers are my favourite, because they were bold enough to follow the North Star, bold enough to answer the ancient call and run towards eternity with no desire to turn back. How could they? When their entire life has led them to this very place. A place where they can hear their souls say; We made it home at long last. They leave their shoes by the door, sip warm tea by the fireplace and sit still for a while, reflecting on the journey so far. They have arrived at a way-station on their way to their final destination and rivers burst from their eyes after all the years of trying to find the Light and then the Light found them when they least expected it. They weep because many didn't make it, many of their comrades had turned back leaving them to walk the path alone. For some the path was too steep, the trenches too deep, the dark times too harsh and fitting in seemed so much easier, so their quest for the Truth became a thing of the past. They weep because the world from which they came had to die for them to give birth to this moment. The sweetness sits in knowing that this is just the beginning of their journey. Oh what a wondrous journey. May we be greeted with the loving embrace of The Most Beautiful One when we arrive at our journey's end.

# Alchemy

I believe in alchemy.
That lead can be transformed
Into gold
Water into wine.
I believe in time
That the tale will unfold
Perfectly.
I believe in destiny
The pen has been lifted
The ink is now dry
On those sacred scrolls
In the sky.
I believe each breath is a seed
We exhale onto a world
Of fertile possibilities.
I believe who we are now
Is not the end of our story
And our reflection in the mirror
Does not always depict
Our true reality.
This world of forms
Is only a shadow of the Truth
The deeper we seek
The higher we rise
If only we knew.
I believe in betterment
In elevation
In expansion
Beyond our dreams.
Inhale (hold)
Exhale (release)
Breathe
Remember the Divinity
Secreted in us
To remind us

We are part celestial
And part dust.
Veiled by our human-ness
We've forgotten who we are
To know yourself
Is to know your Lord
We are envied by the stars.
I believe in the miracles
That exist within our selves
The power of our potential
The revolution in our cells.
I believe sinners can become saints
And saints can fall from grace.
I believe in enlightenment
Whilst sitting on the night train.
I believe our environment
Does not dictate our fate.
I believe the world is mine
As long as I don't get in the way.
I believe in alchemy.
Truly.
Do you?

"And you? When will you begin that long journey into yourself?"

- Jalal ad-Din Muhammad Rumi

You have hidden yourself from the Presence of Allah.
The Presence of Allah is not absent it is Omnipresent
And closer to you than anything else.
If you fail to find this Presence
Then you are the one who is absent
Not the Divine Presence.

- Shaykh Ibrahim Niasse

# Gratitude

In the Name of Allah, The Beneficent, The Compassionate, The Merciful, The Ever-Present, Ever-Near, The Loving, Kind and Generous Lord. All praise is due unto You in every state and all gratitude is due unto You for the gift of this tender heart You have given me and the ability to catch it's overflow in poetry. Thank You for the invitation to seek You, thank You for the courage to pursue nearness and proximity to You, not because I'm perfect, but because a life without You in it is not a life worth living. Thank You for guidance in the form of all of Your Prophets (peace be upon them all) and thank You for the gift of being from the community of the Prophet Muhammed ﷺ. Thank You for allowing me to be from amongst those who strive in the way of loving him, amongst those who strive to follow him in spirit and form. Thank You for giving me the strength to push through my own insecurities and fears to get this collection out, may these words serve a purpose that You are pleased with and may my pleasure lie in what pleases You.

This collection would not have been possible without the unending and unrelenting support of my husband, best friend, confidante, companion on the path, manager and literally my biggest fan Mohammed Yahya. You believe in me when I don't believe in myself, you relieve the weight when everything gets too heavy and I feel overwhelmed by it all. You share the burden with me, hug me tight when I feel weak and let me know everything will be fine. The words are mine but this book exists because of you. Eu te amo com todo o meu coração. May Allah bless with with a reward fitting for your love, support and selflessness. To my mother, my life, my heart, my breath, my reason for being. You are the greatest gift that God has ever gifted me. Your love and care is inconceivable and at times I can't comprehend the level of love you extend. I am grateful for your existence and all your support for anything I have attempted to do in my life. Thank you for giving me the deadline to get this book out, that was exactly what I needed to get into action and finally get these poems into book form. May God continue to bless you and keep you beautiful. To my father for setting out on the journey towards knowledge of self before me and leaving a legacy for me to build upon. Thank you for your unending love and support, we are grateful for your life.

To my Shaykh, my guide, my teacher, the one who points me towards goodness in all things, the one who embodies service to Allah and following in the way of the Messenger ﷺ You encourage me to be the best version of myself and to walk steadily on the path towards God, your tender guidance is like a gentle breeze from heaven, Al Hamdullilah. Shaykh Mouhamadou Mahy Cissé, I don't have enough words to thank Allah for the blessing that you are in my life, so it is sufficient for me to say Al Hamdullilah from now until I breathe my final breath. It is an honour to be your Mureedah. May Allah forever be pleased with you and elevate your state with every breath.

To my Aunty Cutie for being the first person in our family to publish a book, we are so proud of you. To Aunty Omoba for the spiritual insight and guidance throughout my life. To Aunt Viv the artist and Grandma Owen the lover of literature may you rest in perfect peace. To all my grandparents who made the journey from the Caribbean so we could have a better life, we thank you, we salute you, we are you. To my siblings Nyame, Sikelela, Omari and Amon this is for you. To my niece Chaya and nephews Amari and Eli and the little bun that is in the oven right now, Aunty loves you so much. Bless up to all my cousins, too many names to mention, but I love you. To my beautiful in-laws who always show so much love and support for my work especially Mana Sylvia and Mana Joana, I love and appreciate you.

To my soul family, especially the Fetugas, what a blessed and noble family you are MashaAllah, I'm always astonished by the sheer goodness that emanates from your entire family. Thank you for allowing me to be a part of your family, thank you for always keeping your doors open to us, thank you for allowing your home to be the place where we gathered weekly for years to worship Allah and glorify His Name. May Allah reward you abundantly. A special shout out to Rakaya Fetuga for proofreading this collection and Dr Jamillah Karim for to, I am truly grateful. Thank you to Asiya for being the first person to read my collection from beginning to end, I can't explain how it felt to watch you absorb my words. To my UK Tijani family, many of these poems were written after being in your company or inspired by our time together seeking Allah's Face in the city, there are too many names to mention but I thank Allah for you. To the one who sparked my desire to deepen my connection to Allah, I am grateful to Allah for you presence in my life at that moment in time.

To Imam Cheikh Tijani Cissé, the Imam of the Fayda, I am grateful to know you and to be known by you, I am grateful for your limitless hospitality and for offering me a refuge in Medina Baye for me to return to again and again when the weight of the world is too much. Thank you for giving me a home in Africa, a home for my soul. May Allah grant you long life and good health. To Shaykh Khalil Niasse thank you for the knowledge and wisdom your constantly share about the Tariqa and the teachings of Shaykh Ibrahim Niasse and to Sayyidah Aissatou Cissé thank you both for being a piece of Medina Baye in England. Thank you to Cheikh Boukar Niang for giving me my first platform to speak in Medina Baye, for always encouraging my poetry and my academic work and for sharing knowledge about our Grand Shaykh and the noble path we follow.

To my dear teacher Shaykh Babikir, I am so grateful to Allah for you, I have no words to describe what you mean to me. From the first time I met you as a brand new Muslim you encouraged me to continue with my poetry and you have never stopped supporting me and encouraging me to share my words. You are a rare gem, a true saint in the city.

I am grateful that you entrusted me with the managing of Rumi's Cave and trusted my vision for it. Many of these poems were written whilst working at Rumi's Cave, some were literally written in the Cave, I dedicate so much of this work to you and the time spent with you there, in Spain and in Turkey. May Allah extend your life so we can continue to benefit from your presence. To Aminah Babikir and all the people of the Cave, May Allah increase you.

To Muneera Pilgrim, we have walked many roads together and I am truly grateful for the paths we have trod, the art we have made and the stages we have graced together. Although Poetic Pilgrimage no longer exists as a group, all that I am is as a result of PP and our pure intentions to make music to elevate our people, I salute the younger us, we had enough fire to keep the whole world warm. I appreciate you.

To my Muslim family, to all the lovers of Rasullulah ﷺ, to my Tijani and Fayda family across the globe, I appreciate you all so much, thank you for the prayers and your support. To all my family in Medina Baye, you have my heart. To my brother Amir Sulaiman for being a remarkable poet and role model, may Allah preserve your pen and increase you in all that is good in this life and the next. To the Beloveds, my sisters, my tribe, I am so grateful that Allah has gathered me with believing women to journey together on the path to Him. In these times of darkness, you sisters are my light. I thank Allah for you. To my tribe that I haven't met yet, I already love you.

To all those who have come to my performances who have shared a good word afterwards, to all who shed a tear, to all who gave me hugs after shows, to all who encouraged me to continue, to those who shared my poems on their social media platforms, liked a post and recommended my words to their family and friends, I truly, truly appreciate you. To all who have attended my courses, I appreciate you so much for journeying with me. I would like to thank Valentina for the cover art, I am so pleased with what you have created my love, you took my ideas and created magic, I am in love with it.

Thank you Allah for absolutely everything. Al Hamdullilah, always.

# Glossary

**Abaya (Arabic):** A loose over-garment worn by Muslim women.

**Ahadun Ahad (Arabic):** Literally *One, One* referring to the Oneness of God. A statement proclaimed by Bilal ibn Ribah a companion of the Prophet Muhammed ﷺ.

**Al Hamdullilah (Arabic):** Literally *praise be to God* or *all praise is due to God.*

**Allah (Arabic):** The Arabic word for God. The name Allah is used by Arabic speaking people of different religions.

**Ansari (Arabic):** Literally *helper* referring to the citizens of Medina that helped the Prophet Muhammad ﷺ after he migrated from Mecca.

**Ashadu an lā ilāha illa -llāhu wa- ashadu anna muhammadan rasūlu-llāh (Arabic):** *I bear witness that there is no deity but God, and I bear witness that Muhammad is the messenger of God.* A sincere utterance of this sentence is all that is required for a person to become a Muslim

**Asma ul Husna (Arabic):** Literally *The Beautiful Names*, referring to the Names of God mentioned in the Quran.

**Barhama:** A name derived from the Arabic name Ibrahim popular in West Africa. Used to refer to Senegalese scholar, mystic and poet; Shaykh Ibrahim Niasse.

**Deen (Arabic):** Religion or the way of life of the Muslims.

**Dhikr (Arabic):** Literally *remembrance, reminder* or *mention* and is used in this context to mean remembrance of God.

**Dhul Hijjah (Arabic):** The twelfth month in the Islamic Calendar. It is one of the sacred months, in this month Muslims perform the Hajj Pilgrimage to Mecca.

**Dunya (Arabic):** Refers to the temporal realm, this lower world.

**Fa Inni Qareeb (Arabic):** Literally *Indeed I am Near.*

**Habibullah (Arabic):** *Beloved of God*, a name ascribed to the Prophet Muhammed ﷺ.

**Hashimi (Arabic):** A member or descendant of the Banu Hashim clan of the Quraysh tribe that the Prophet Muhammed was a member of.

**Jannat al Baqi (Arabic):** an Islamic cemetery in Medina, located to the southeast of the Prophet's Mosque.

**Jita Sharaftal Madina Marhaban Ya Khayra Da (Arabic):** *You have brought to this city nobleness, Welcome best caller to God's way.* Lyrics from famous Islamic hymn Tala'a Al-Badru 'Alayna.

**Kaolack (Wolof):** A town in Senegal on the north bank of the Saloum River which borders The Gambia. Within Kaolack is Medina Baye, a Sufi village founded by Shaykh Ibrahim Niasse.

**Ka'aba (Arabic):** A building at the centre of Islam's most holy mosque in Mecca, Saudi Arabia. Considered by Muslims to be the House of God, it is the direction of prayer for Muslims around the world.

**La Ilaha il Allah (Arabic):** Literally *There is no god but God.* In Islamic spirituality it is understood to mean there is no reality but the True Reality of God.

**Maghrib (Arabic):** Referring to one of the five prayers that the Muslims perform daily, Maghrib is the sunset prayer.

**Madinat-un Nabi (Arabic):** *The City of the Prophet,* referring to Medina in Saudi Arabia where the Prophet Muhammed ﷺ is buried.

**Madani (Arabic):** Literally *of Medina,* referring to Medina in Saudi Arabia

**Masjid (Arabic):** Literally *place of prostration.* Commonly referred to as a Mosque

**Masjid an-Nabawi (Arabic):** The Prophet's Mosque in Medina in Saudi Arabia

**Maulana (Arabic):** Literally *our master.* A title preceding the name of respected religious leader, referring to Jalal ad-Din Muhammad Rumi.

**Medina al Munawarra (Arabic):** The Illuminated City, referring to Medina in Saudi Arabia.

**Melfha (Arabic):** A Saharan garment worn by women.

**Minka Ilayka (Arabic):** Literally *from you to you.*

**Mureedah (Arabic):** A female seeker, who has committed to Sufi path under the guidance of a Shaykh.

**Mustapha (Arabic):** Literally *The Chosen One*, one of the names of the Prophet Muhammed ﷺ.

**Nabi (Arabic):** Prophet.

**Nabi ar Rahma (Arabic):** Prophet of Mercy.

**Nafs (Arabic):** Literally *self*. The nafs in its unrefined state is similar to the concept of the ego which is considered to be the lowest aspect of a human's nature.

**Noor (Arabic):** Light.

**Oud (Arabic):** Literally *wood*, referring Oud chips used as a form of incense.

**Qari (Arabic):** A reciter of the Quran

**Quran (Arabic):** The central religious text of Islam, believed by Muslims to be a direct revelation from Allah, revealed by Allah to the Prophet Muhammed ﷺ through the archangel Gabriel.

**Rabbil Alameen (Arabic):** Lord of the Worlds.

**Ramadan (Arabic):** The ninth month of the Islamic calendar, observed by Muslims worldwide as a month of fasting, prayer, reflection and community.

**Rasullulah (Arabic):** Messenger of Allah

**Rabia al Adawiyyah:** A female saint, poet and mystic from Basra in Iraq. Born in the 8th century.

**Rumi:** Referring to Jalāl al-Dīn Muḥammad Rūmī, a 13th-century poet, scholar, theologian and Sufi mystic originally from Greater Khorasan in Greater Iran, buried in Konya, Turkey.

**Salatul Fatihi (Arabic):** A prayer for the Prophet Muhammed ﷺ that makes up a regular part of the litany practiced individually or in congregation by followers of the Tijaniyyah Sufi order.

**Salatul Janaza (Arabic):** Islamic Funeral Prayer.

**Salawat an-Nabi (Arabic):** Prayers upon the Prophet ﷺ.

**Sayyidina (Arabic):** Literally our master.

**Shams at-Tabriz:** Also Shams al-Din Mohammad, a Persian poet who is credited as the spiritual instructor of Rumi.

**Shaykh ul Murabbi (Arabic):** A Sufi Shaykh and guide who teaches the student the necessary etiquette on the path towards Allah.

**Taha (Arabic):** A name that is is the combination of two letters considered to be amongst the mysteriously revealed letters in the Quran whose meaning is unknown. Also TaHa is One of the names of the Prophet Muhammed ﷺ

**Tawwaf (Arabic):** The act of circling the Ka'aba counterclockwise, part of the rites for the completion of the pilgrimages.

**Wali (Arabic):** Friend, in this instance referring to a Friend of God, a term similar to the Christian concept of a saint.

**Ya Awwal (Arabic):** Literally *O, The First One* referring to one of the 99 Names of Allah. Al Awwal means The One whose Existence is without a beginning. He is truly the first and nothing was before Him.

**Ya Akhir (Arabic):** Literally *O, The Last One* referring to one of the 99 Names of Allah. Al Akhir is The One whose Existence is without an end, whose existence will extend past the end of this universe.

**Ya Baatin (Arabic):** Literally *O, The Hidden One* referring to one of the 99 Names of Allah. Al Baatin is The One who is hidden or secret. Allah is unseen but His Existence is known through His signs.

**Ya Rahman:** Literally *O, The Beneficent One* referring to one of the 99 Names of Allah. Ar Rahman is the One who is most merciful, kind, and loving towards all creation. His mercy and embraces all.

**Ya Zahir (Arabic):** Literally *O, The Manifest One* referring to one of the 99 Names of Allah. Al Zahir is The One who is evident and conspicuous. He made Himself evident without being visible.

**Zam Zam (Arabic):** The Zam Zam well is located Mecca, Saudi Arabia and is believed to be a miraculously generated source of water which sprang thousands of years ago.

**و (Arabic):** Arabic letter for W

**ﷺ (Arabic):** Peace be upon him. A prayer that Muslims say after mentioning the name of the Prophet Muhammed ﷺ

# SUKINA

### N O O R

Printed in Great Britain
by Amazon